Tasty Steamer Recipes

Everyday Meals

Must-Try Steamer Dishes for Breakfast-Lunch-Dinner

BY

MOLLY MILLS

Copyright © 2020 by Molly Mills

License Notes

No part of this book may be copied, replicated, distributed, sold or shared without the express and written consent of the Author.

The ideas expressed in the book are for entertainment purposes. The Reader assumes all risk when following any guidelines and the Author accepts no responsibility if damages occur due to actions taken by the Reader.

Table of Contents

Introduction 6

Steaming: A Delightful Way to Cook 9

Breakfast Favorites 11

    Steamed Eggs 12

    Steamed Oatmeal 14

    Steamed Pork Buns 16

    Steamed Sausage Biscuit 20

    Steamed Breakfast Bread 22

Lunch & Dinner Picks 24

    Steamed Sweet Potatoes in Green Onion Vinaigrette 25

    Steamed Artichokes with Lemon Butter Sauce 27

    Steamed Green Beans in Shallot Vinaigrette 29

    Steamed Broccoli 31

    Steamed Veggies with Chile-Lime Sauce 33

    Asian-Style Steamed Vegetables 35

    Steamed Vegetable Salad 37

Ginger-Soy Steamed Sea Bass 39

Steamed Prawns in Garlic Sauce 42

Steamed Mussels 44

Chinese-Style Steamed Fish 46

Steamed Lobster 49

Mediterranean-Style Steamed Salmon 51

Steamed Scallops 54

Thai-Style Steamed Barramundi Fish 56

Steamed Shellfish Pot 59

Steamed Lemon-Garlic Chicken 62

Steamed Beef with Oyster Sauce 64

Steamed Pork Ribs and Pumpkin 67

Steamed Meat Dumplings 69

Steamed Minced Pork 72

Chinese-Style Steamed Chicken 75

Steamed Carrot Cake 78

Steamed Sponge Cake 81

Steamed Chocolate Cake 84

Conclusion 87

About the Author 88

Don't Miss Out! 89

Introduction

Steaming is one of the most amazing of conventional cooking techniques. It helps to maximize the taste of the food through the application of moist heat while maintaining their vibrant colors so they look fresh and appetizing. It is also one of the healthiest ways to cook your food, sans the need for oil. Other than that, it has also been proven to retain as many nutrients in meats and fish and veggies along the way.

Steaming is pretty simple but it can make a huge difference, especially in making sure that you enjoy the full experience of the distinctive flavors of the food, no matter what you throw into it. Here are 30 recipes to prove that no matter how times may have changed and how cooking endured technological advancements, steaming remains timeless, and definitely a useful cooking method to master – if you want to serve really good food. Check out the listing:

Breakfast Favorites:

- Steamed Eggs
- Steamed Oatmeal
- Steamed Pork Buns
- Steamed Sausage Biscuit
- Steamed Breakfast Bread

Lunch and Dinner Picks:

- Steamed Sweet Potatoes in Green Onion Vinaigrette
- Steamed Artichokes with Lemon Butter Sauce
- Steamed Green Beans in Shallot Vinaigrette
- Steamed Broccoli
- Steamed Veggies with Chile-Lime Sauce
- Asian-Style Steamed Vegetables
- Steamed Vegetable Salad
- Ginger-Soy Steamed Sea Bass
- Steamed Prawns in Garlic Sauce
- Steamed Mussels
- Chinese-Style Steamed Fish

- Steamed Lobster
- Mediterranean-Style Steamed Salmon
- Steamed Scallops
- Thai-Style Steamed Barramundi Fish
- Steamed Shellfish Pot
- Steamed Lemon-Garlic Chicken
- Steamed Beef with Oyster Sauce
- Steamed Pork Ribs and Pumpkin
- Steamed Meat Dumplings
- Steamed Minced Pork
- Chinese-Style Steamed Chicken
- Steamed Carrot Cake
- Steamed Sponge Cake
- Steamed Chocolate Cake

We hope we made the point clear enough: the steamer is unbelievably useful. You must have one around the house to cook delicious family food at different times of the day.

Steaming: A Delightful Way to Cook

Steaming is one of the oldest of the cooking methods. It's a natural way of cooking food in the most healthful manner possible. It helps you to cook food without making the color dull. It is also a great way to maximize the full essence of the food, so you enjoy the best flavor experience with every serving.

Steaming is basically a moist heat method wherein food is cooked through the steam that comes out when boiled water vaporizes, without needing to submerge it directly onto the hot liquid. All that you need to do to cook food is to keep it in close contact with the hot steam as much as possible. That's why steamers have lids. You need to keep the moist heat trapped.

Steaming is applicable if you want your food to come out light and healthy because there will be no need for oil or butter or any kind of grease – for the most part. And yeah, there are a lot of food ingredients that are good with the steamer. You can actually make tasty and healthy dishes off a variety of meat, fish, vegetables, and others without the sweat.

Mind you; it does not take very long to cook food in the steamer. Sometimes, all you need is a few minutes to an hour to make sure it is done. Telling signs depend on what you are cooking. On several occasions, there may be time limits to follow, or you need to check if the food is tender or if the vegetables are already bright in color. It is very important that you follow instructions and you keep watch on your food while you are steaming. Overcooking can make your food mushy and tasteless, at the very least.

Here are additional tips to make sure your steamer recipes emerge nothing but delicious!

- Keep the lid on. This is the key trick to maintain the heat level needed to cook your food and maintain the water level at the bottom of the pan. The lid must be airtight to ensure that hot steam will actually touch your food because that's what will cook it through.
- Let the water boil before putting the steamer basket in. Never throw everything in one go before you turn on the cooker or the stove, whichever you might be using. The food simply tastes better when you bring the water to a rolling boil first.
- Once the boiling point is reached, you can reduce heat from high to medium. But make sure you do not turn down the heat too much. Otherwise, you will stop creating the steam or the amount of moist heat needed to cook the food.
- Make sure that the boiling water does not touch the food as it boils. The water level must always be below the steamer basket. One or two inches of water from the bottom of the pot is most ideal. You could always add water as needed because you would not want to let it all evaporate and burn the pan before you are done cooking.
- Although most recipes would only ask you to add water to the bottom of the pan, nothing is preventing you from being creative. You can actually add herbs and a stock cube into the water to infuse a hint of flavor into the steam.
- Do not overcook your food. Steaming sometimes requires that you check on your food regularly for doneness. You do not want it overcooked and dry and tasteless.

Steaming is a wonderful way to prepare food for the family. Don't get overwhelmed. This is just a simple cooking technique that is easy to learn and easy enough to master. So, let's get the boil rolling, and let's start steaming!

Breakfast Favorites

Steamed Eggs

There are many ways to cook eggs and enjoy them for breakfast. Steaming eggs is a great way to enjoy them, as taught to us by Asian cooks. The Korean, Chinese, and Japanese cuisine are among those that developed special steamed egg recipes to the delight of the rest of the world. The result is a silky and savory dish that seems like a real treat early in the morning.

Serving Size: 2

Prep Time: 20 mins

Ingredients:

- 2 pcs large eggs
- ½ pc scallion, chopped
- ¼ tsp sesame seeds, toasted
- ½ cup water
- ¼ tsp salt

Instructions:

1. Prepare the steamer, placing water at the pot halfway and boiling it on medium fire.

2. Whisk together eggs, water, and salt in a heat-proof bowl until foamy.

3. Place the bowl into the steamer basket and cover with the lid. Let it cook for about 12 minutes.

4. After 12 minutes, sprinkle scallions and toasted sesame seeds on top of the eggs and cook for 3 more minutes.

5. Serve hot.

Steamed Oatmeal

For health-conscious individuals, oatmeal is the go-to breakfast. It's healthy, packed with nutrients, and low in calories. If you want to try something for your oats, place them in the steamer. This way, you will be able to enjoy non-gummy oats that are truly delightful!

Serving Size: 2

Prep Time: 15 mins

Ingredients:

- ¾ cup old-fashioned oats
- Salt to taste

Instructions:

1. Place enough water in a pot and boil over medium fire.

2. Place oats in a fine mesh or coriander and set onto the steamer.

3. Let it steam for about 10 minutes.

4. Sprinkle with salt to taste and serve.

Steamed Pork Buns

Steamed Pork Buns are a fast-food favorite. They are the perfect food-to-go and delicious comfort food, which you can well have any mealtime of the day. Serving them for breakfast; however, it seems like a good idea because they are tasty and filling and great enough to start your day.

Serving Size: 5

Prep Time: 2 hrs. 40 mins

Ingredients:

For the dough

- 11oz all-purpose flour
- 2 tbsp sugar
- ½ tsp Kosher salt
- 1 tsp baking powder
- 1 tsp instant dry yeast
- 1 tbsp vegetable oil
- ¾ cup water

For the filling

- 2 pcs dried shiitake mushrooms, soaked in ½ cup water
- 1 pc green onion, thinly sliced
- 4 pcs cabbage leaves, thinly sliced
- 1 tsp Kosher salt
- ¾ lb. ground pork
- 1 tbsp ginger, peeled and grated
- 1 tsp sugar
- 1 tbsp sake
- 1 tbsp soy sauce
- 1 tbsp roasted sesame oil
- 1 tbsp cornstarch
- Freshly ground black pepper to taste

Instructions:

1. Mix together flour, oil, baking powder, yeast, 2 tablespoons of sugar, and ½ teaspoon of salt in a large bowl.

2. Slowly add water, stirring as you go, until the mixture is incorporated.

3. Work the dough in a lightly floured surface and knead until the dough is silky and smooth, about 15 minutes.

4. Transfer dough to a bowl, cover with cling wrap, and set aside at room temperature for 30 minutes to an hour or until it doubles in size.

5. Meanwhile, make the filling.

6. Sprinkle the remaining salt onto cabbage, squeeze out the liquid and place in a large bowl.

7. Drain mushrooms and chop, then, add into the bowl with cabbage.

8. Add pork, ginger, scallions, and the rest of the ingredients. Mix everything thoroughly until well blended.

9. When the dough is ready, work the dough again in a lightly floured work surface. Divide it in half and form each into a log.

10. Divide the logs evenly into 10 pieces each, arrange in a baking tray, and cover with plastic wrap. Set aside again to rest for about 10 minutes.

11. Working with each piece at a time, roll the dough and flatten to make a thin round shape.

12. Spoon about a tablespoon and a half of prepared filling into the middle and form it into a bun, making sure the filling is tucked neatly. Repeat until all the buns are filled.

13. Arrange filled buns in another baking tray lined with cut parchment paper, cover with another sheet of plastic wrap and set aside for about 20 minutes.

14. When the buns are almost ready, bring enough water to boil in the bottom of a steamer pot on medium high heat.

15. Arrange the buns, together with the parchment paper bottom, in the steamer tray. Make sure that you leave about 2 inches of space between each.

16. Steam buns for about 10 minutes per batch.

17. Serve warm and enjoy. You may also keep leftover buns in the fridge, placed in a tight container. Reheat in the steamer when you are ready to serve.

Steamed Sausage Biscuit

Sausage biscuits are delightful. But did you know you can further level up its place in the yummy meter by simply skipping the oven and using the steamer instead to cook the biscuits? Well, yes, you can! Enjoy this as a delightful, tasty, and healthy breakfast or brunch meal and you will not regret it. That's a promise!

Serving Size: 6

Prep Time: 15 mins

Ingredients:

- 6 pcs biscuit dough, presliced
- 6 pcs sausage patties, cooked
- 6 pcs cheese slices

Instructions:

1. Boil enough water in a steamer pot.

2. Prepare the tray, line with precut parchment paper, leaving about 2 inches of space in between.

3. Place the biscuit dough on the tray and steam for about 10 minutes or until cooked through.

4. To assemble the biscuit, lay down a piece of dough, top with cooked sausage and a piece of cheese slice and cover with another piece of dough.

5. Serve and enjoy.

Steamed Breakfast Bread

For those who don't like something heavy for breakfast, bread is the way to go. But you don't always need freshly baked bread to greet you a good morning. Sometimes, a steamed variation can do it as well. Here is a wonderful breakfast bread you should thank your steamer for. Let's have a start!

Serving Size: 4

Prep Time: 20 mins

Ingredients:

- 1 cup cake flour
- 1 cup milk
- 1 tsp baking powder
- 2 tbsp sugar

Instructions:

1. Combine cake flour, baking powder, and sugar in a large bowl.

2. Slowly stir in milk until incorporated.

3. Pour batter into plastic or silicone molds.

4. Arrange the molds in the steamer tray, then, boil enough water in the pot over medium fire.

5. Place the steamer tray on top and let it cook for about 10 minutes.

6. Serve and enjoy.

Lunch & Dinner Picks

Steamed Sweet Potatoes in Green Onion Vinaigrette

Sweet potatoes are some tasty hunger busters, and they are healthy, too. Get a grip with this delectable meal that's quick and easy to make and easy enough to please the palate. The seasoned sweet potatoes would pass up as a light lunch or dinner or a handsome side dish for you and the entire family.

Serving Size: 4

Prep Time: 35 mins

Ingredients:

- 2 pcs sweet potatoes, quartered and scored
- ½ cup green onion, chopped
- 1 cup cilantro leaves, chopped
- 3 cloves garlic, chopped
- 3 tbsp seasoned rice wine vinegar
- 1 tbsp fish sauce
- ¼ tsp chili paste
- ¼ cup vegetable oil

Instructions:

1. Boil water into the steamer pot over medium fire.

2. Add sweet potatoes into the steamer tray and place over the pot. Let it cook for about 20 minutes or until tender.

3. Meanwhile, heat oil in a pan over medium fire and sauté garlic for about 1 minute.

4. Stir in green onions, plus vinegar, chili paste, and fish sauce.

5. Toss in chopped cilantro and cook for a minute more.

6. To assemble, arrange sweet potatoes in a platter, then, spoon over prepared vinaigrette.

7. Serve and enjoy.

Steamed Artichokes with Lemon Butter Sauce

Artichokes are best-tasting when steamed. Why? They retain their bright color and much of their nutrients when they are steamed. And they taste so delicious, especially if you pair up the artichokes with some lemon butter sauce.

Serving Size: 4

Prep Time: 40 mins

Ingredients:

- 4 pcs artichokes, trimmed
- ½ cup butter
- 2 tbsp lemon juice
- 1 tbsp parsley, minced

Instructions:

1. Boil enough water in the steamer pot over medium fire.

2. Place artichokes, bottoms up, in the steamer tray and into the pot. Let it cook for about half an hour.

3. Meanwhile, make the lemon butter sauce by whisking together melted butter, lemon juice, and parsley in a bowl.

4. Place artichokes in a platter and serve with lemon butter sauce on the side.

Steamed Green Beans in Shallot Vinaigrette

Green beans are great as a side dish to any dinner meal. And there is no better way to prepare green beans than steaming. Serve it with a shallot vinaigrette and give your palate some real treat. This is light, tasty, and truly delicious. You will enjoy it with every bite.

Serving Size: 4

Prep Time: 20 mins

Ingredients:

- 12oz green beans, trimmed
- 1 pc shallot, minced
- 1 tsp Dijon mustard
- 1 tbsp red wine vinegar
- ¼ cup extra-virgin olive oil

Kosher salt and freshly ground black pepper to taste

Instructions:

1. Boil enough water in a steamer pot over medium fire.

2. Place beans in a steamer tray and into the pot and cook for about 10 minutes.

3. Meanwhile, stir together shallots, mustard, vinegar, and oil. Season with salt and pepper and mix to blend.

4. Toss steamed green beans with the prepared shallot vinaigrette.

5. Place in a sealed container and marinade for about an hour or overnight in the fridge before serving.

Steamed Broccoli

Broccoli is one of the most amazing vegetables that sit well with the steamer. By steaming, you will be able to retain the bright green color of the veggie and all of its nutrients. They also do not require much to please. Simply serve freshly steamed broccoli florets with a mixture of garlic, oil, and lemon juice, and you have got a delicious meal.

Serving Size: 2

Prep Time: 10 mins

Ingredients:

- ¾ lb. broccoli, separated into florets
- 1 clove garlic, minced
- 1 ½ tsp lemon juice
- 1 ½ tbsp olive oil
- Salt and pepper to taste

Instructions:

1. Boil enough water in the steamer pot over medium fire.

2. Add broccoli florets into the steamer tray and cook for about 5 minutes or until crisp-tender.

3. Meanwhile, heat oil in a saucepan and sauté garlic until lightly browned.

4. Stir in lemon juice and season with some salt and pepper to taste.

5. Toss broccoli with garlic mixture and serve.

Steamed Veggies with Chile-Lime Sauce

For some real veg fest, you can combine different vegetables, pop them into the steamer tray and steam away. This recipe can be done well in the wok. But since this is a steamer cookbook and we are aiming for the healthiest meal, we are dropping the oil (although we will need some for the sauce) and going for some steam.

Serving Size: 4

Prep Time: 15 mins

Ingredients:

- ¼ pc broccoli head, separated into florets
- ¼ pc cauliflower head, separated into florets
- 8 pcs asparagus spears, cut into 2-inch pieces
- 3 pcs carrots, peeled and sliced into ½-inch pieces
- 2 garlic cloves, chopped
- 1 tbsp sesame-chile oil
- 1 tsp olive oil
- Juice of ½ pc lemon
- ¼ tsp red pepper flakes
- Kosher salt and freshly ground black pepper to taste

Instructions:

1. Boil enough water in a steamer pot over medium fire.

2. Toss the veggies in the steamer tray or a metal steamer basket and steam for about 5 minutes, until crisp-tender.

3. Meanwhile, heat sesame-chili oil and olive oil in a saucepan.

4. Sauté garlic for about a minute, then, sprinkle with red pepper flakes and some salt and pepper.

5. Transfer steamed veggies into a large serving bowl, stir in sesame-chile mixture, plus lemon juice, and adjust seasoning as needed.

6. Serve and enjoy.

Asian-Style Steamed Vegetables

Here is another version of the steamed veggies. This time, we are bathing the crisp-tender vegetables in a delectable Asian sauce. If you have access to one, and to make this dish authentic, use a bamboo steamer for this recipe. That will help you get a dish that's closest to the original.

Serving Size: 4

Prep Time: 20 mins

Ingredients:

- 3 cups broccoli, separated into florets
- 3 cups cauliflower, separated into florets
- 14oz carrots, cut into strips
- 8oz green beans, trimmed and halved
- 12oz zucchini, cut into strips
- 4 pcs baby bok choy, quartered
- 2 tsp rice wine
- 2 tbsp sweet soy sauce
- 1 ½ tbsp oyster sauce
- 1 tsp sesame oil

Instructions:

1. Boil enough water in a wok over medium fire.

2. Toss broccoli and cauliflower florets, plus carrots and green beans, in a bamboo steamer basket.

3. Place the bamboo steamer on the wok and let it cook for 2 minutes.

4. Add zucchini and bok choy in another bamboo steamer basket and place on top of the first one.

5. Continue to cook for another 3 minutes until all of the veggies are crisp-tender.

6. In a small bowl, whisk together rice wine, soy sauce, oyster sauce, and sesame oil until well combined.

7. Toss steamed veggies with prepared sauce and serve.

Steamed Vegetable Salad

Do you want a veggie salad that's ultra-healthy and clean? This is the recipe for you. The nice thing about this dish is you can choose any seasonal vegetable that you like and mix and match them the way you want. As long as you have lots of bright colors on the plate, you are doing it good.

Serving Size: 6

Prep Time: 35 mins

Ingredients:

- 4 cups broccoli florets
- 2 pcs carrots, peeled and julienned
- 1 cup green beans, cut into 2-inch strips
- 9oz spinach, trimmed
- 1 tbsp fresh cilantro, coarsely chopped
- ½ cup dry roasted peanuts, finely chopped
- 2 tbsp ginger root, grated
- ½ tsp soy sauce
- 1 tbsp fish sauce
- 2 tbsp sesame oil
- 1 tsp sugar
- ¼ tsp salt

Instructions:

1. Boil enough water in a steamer pot over medium fire.

2. Add broccoli, carrots, and green beans in the steamer tray and steam for 5 minutes.

3. Scatter spinach on top and cook for 2 more minutes.

4. Meanwhile, stir together fish and soy sauce, plus sesame oil, sugar and salt until the solids are dissolved.

5. Once the vegetables are ready, toss in a large bowl together with prepared sauce.

6. Garnish with roasted peanuts and freshly chopped cilantro before serving.

Ginger-Soy Steamed Sea Bass

Moving on from steamed veggies, we are now in the seafood section of this steamer cookbook. Fish, shellfish, and other seafood are another set of delectable ingredients that sit well with the steamer. Through steaming, they retain their flavors and they get that bright color, which looks so amazing at the dining table.

Serving Size: 4

Prep Time: 25 mins

Ingredients:

- 2 pcs whole sea bass, cleaned
- ⅓ cup ginger, peeled and julienned
- ½ cup ginger, peeled and sliced
- 4 pcs green onions, julienned
- 1 tbsp cornstarch
- 3 tsp sugar
- ½ cup soy sauce
- ¼ cup vegetable oil

Instructions:

1. Boil enough water in a steamer pot over medium fire.

2. Place a metal trivet or a heat-proof plate in the steamer tray or on top of the boiling water. Just make sure that the water does not touch the trivet.

3. Meanwhile, coat fish in cornstarch on all sides, then, stuff the insides with ginger slices.

4. Scatter green onions on the trivet, then, place the fish on top.

5. Cover with a lid and let it steam for about 15 minutes or until the fish is opaque and cooked through.

6. Meanwhile, heat oil in a pan over medium fire and sauté julienned ginger.

7. Whisk together soy sauce and sugar in a small bowl until the sugar is dissolved, then, add the mixture into the pan. Let it simmer and turn off fire.

8. When the fish is cooked, carefully lift it from the trivet and place in a serving platter, discarding the ginger slices.

9. Pour prepared sauce into the fish, garnish with more julienned ginger and green onions, and serve.

Steamed Prawns in Garlic Sauce

Now, here is a no-fuss seafood recipe that you will surely adore. It is steamed prawns bathed in a yummy garlic sauce. The name itself of the recipe is mouthwatering, wait till you are able to have a bite. The prawns are plump and fresh, and the sauce simply makes every bite a tasty adventure like no other.

Serving Size: 4

Prep Time: 25 mins

Ingredients:

- 5 pcs tiger prawns, peeled, deveined and halved
- 1 ½ cups garlic, chopped
- 2 pcs spring onions, chopped
- 1 cup vegetable oil

Instructions:

1. Heat oil in a pan over medium fire and sauté garlic until lightly browned.

2. Remove garlic from the oil with a slotted spoon, then, set aside to cool down.

3. Coat prawns in garlic and arrange in a steamer tray.

4. Boil enough water in a steamer pot over medium fire and put the steamer tray with the prawns once it is already boiling.

5. Steam the prawns for about 5 minutes or until bright orange in color.

6. To serve, place the prawns in a serving platter and garnish with more sautéed garlic, plus chopped spring onions.

Steamed Mussels

Mussels are delightful, and they are perfect for steaming! You only need a few minutes to enjoy your mussels. Pair them with a delicious sauce, and you will surely enjoy mealtime the best way. This dish is best served with some toasted bread or even rice if you are a rice person.

Serving Size: 4

Prep Time: 10 mins

Ingredients:

- 2 lbs. mussels, trimmed and rinsed
- 1/3 cup parsley leaves, chopped
- 2 tbsp garlic, minced
- 1-12oz bottle pale ale
- ½ cup tahini
- ½ cup clam juice

Instructions:

1. Place beer, clam juice, tahini, and garlic in a steamer pot and boil on high.

2. Add mussels to a steamer tray and into the pot. Let it cook in a steam for about 5 minutes or until the mussels open.

3. Serve with a garnish of freshly chopped parsley.

Chinese-Style Steamed Fish

Steaming fish is very prominent in Chinese cuisine. It is a highly favored cooking method because after placing the fish in the steamer, there are a lot of things you can do to flare up the flavors of the dish and make it super delicious. The aromatic sauce in this recipe is just one example of how the Chinese cooks do it, and it's worth emulating because it tastes real good.

Serving Size: 2

Prep Time: 30 mins

Ingredients:

- 1 lb. head-on sea bass, rinsed, scaled, and gutted
- 1 tbsp ginger, sliced
- ½ tbsp ginger, julienned
- 1 cup green onions, chopped
- 2 pcs dried chili peppers
- ½ tsp Sichuan peppercorn
- 2 tbsp rice wine
- 2 tbsp seasoned soy sauce
- 1 tbsp peanut oil
- 1 tsp sesame oil

Instructions:

1. Boil enough water in a wok over medium fire.

2. Meanwhile, prepare the fish.

3. Scatter ¼ cup of green onions in a plate that is large enough to carry the fish but could still fit into a metal steamer basket.

4. Rub sesame oil all over the fish, then, stuff another ¼ cup of green onions into its cavity, along with the sliced ginger.

5. Scatter most of the remaining chopped green onions to cover the fish, then, pour in rice wine.

6. Once the water in the wok starts to boil, place the metal steamer basket on the wok, careful for the boiling water not to touch the bottom of the basket.

7. Place the plate down into the metal basket and cover with a lid. Let it cook for about 8 minutes or until the fish is cooked through.

8. Meanwhile, heat peanut oil in a small pan over medium fire and sauté chili peppers and peppercorns until fragrant.

9. When fish is cooked, transfer to a serving platter, discard any green onions and ginger stuffed into the fish.

10. Pour in hot oil straight into the fish so it sizzles, then, add a drizzle of seasoned soy sauce and garnish with the last of the green onions and the julienned ginger.

11. Serve while still warm.

Steamed Lobster

You hardly need anything else if you have steamed lobster at the table. You can eat it and enjoy it and satisfy yourself with every delicious bite. Why steam lobsters? Steaming helps you enjoy the freshness of your catch minus the fishy taste.

Serving Size: 8

Prep Time: 30 mins

Ingredients:

- 8 pcs lobsters
- Fresh water
- Sea salt to taste

Instructions:

1. Boil enough water in a large steamer pot on high heat.

2. Add enough salt into the water to make it taste close to the seawater.

3. Carefully arrange the lobsters into the steamer basket and place it on top of the pot. Cover with a lid and let it steam for about 15 minutes or until cooked through.

4. Serve and enjoy.

Mediterranean-Style Steamed Salmon

Here is another steamed fish recipe that you will adore. This is perfect for your lunch or dinner and would be a great meal to fill your tummy with goodness. The fresh herbs give it a spectacular flavor profile. And since the fish is steamed, you can expect a healthy, moist, and tender bite. Pair it with a plate of your favorite veggie salad, and you are ready for a great, completely satisfying meal.

Serving Size: 4

Prep Time: 25 mins

Ingredients:

- 1 pc yellow onion, halved and sliced
- 4 pcs green onions, trimmed, sliced lengthwise, and divided
- 1 lb. skin-on salmon fillet
- Kosher salt and freshly ground black pepper to taste
- 1 tsp ground coriander
- 1 tsp ground cumin
- ½ tsp Aleppo pepper
- 5 cloves garlic, chopped
- 1 tbsp extra virgin olive oil
- ½ cup fresh parsley leaves, chopped
- 1 pc lemon, thinly sliced
- ½ cup white wine

Instructions:

1. Boil enough water in a steamer pot on medium-high fire.

2. Cut a sheet of parchment or wax paper and place it in a steamer basket.

3. Scatter sliced yellow onions and some of the green onions at the parchment paper and arrange salmon on top.

4. Sprinkle with salt and pepper.

5. In a small bowl, stir together ground cumin and coriander, plus Aleppo pepper.

6. Rub the spice mix into the salmon and then drizzle with half of the olive oil.

7. Cover the top of the salmon with the remaining green onions, plus garlic and freshly chopped parsley, reserving some for garnish.

8. Drizzle the remaining oil and pour in wine.

9. Fold the parchment to enclose the fish, then, cover the steamer basket with a tight fitting lid.

10. Steam for about 5-8 minutes or until the salmon is cooked through

11. Serve and enjoy.

Steamed Scallops

Scallops are another delightful seafood that would turn into a great dish that you could serve as a side dish or even as a main dish. These dressed-up scallops look amazing at a party buffet table. You can serve this to your next shindig and impress your guests, from the look to its taste.

Serving Size: 2

Prep Time: 20 mins

Ingredients:

- 8 pcs large sea scallops
- 4 cloves garlic, crushed
- ¼ tsp chili powder
- 1 pc lemon, sliced into wedges
- 2 tsp lemon juice

Instructions:

1. Boil enough water in a steamer pot over medium fire.

2. Meanwhile, marinade scallops in garlic, chili powder, and lemon juice. Stir well.

3. Transfer scallops into a steamer tray lined with parchment paper and steam for about 10 minutes.

4. Serve and enjoy.

Thai-Style Steamed Barramundi Fish

Here is a refreshing steamed fish recipe. It's made of Barramundi bathed in a tasty Thai-style sauce. It's a perfectly balanced dish with a bit of spice and sourness. There's also a hint of garlic, which will easily offer your dining table a lot more excitement than you imagine. Everyone would love to partake in this dish, an adventure to the palate in every bite.

Serving Size: 4

Prep Time: 35 mins

Ingredients:

For the fish:

- 4 lbs. whole barramundi, rinsed, scaled, gutted, and scored
- 5 pcs lemongrass stalks, smashed and cut into chunks

For the sauce / soup:

- 1 cup chicken stock
- 2 tbsp palm sugar, finely chopped
- 8 tbsp lime juice
- 6 tbsp fish sauce
- 2 heads garlic, chopped
- 3 pcs Thai chilies, finely chopped
- 20 pcs cilantro sprigs, chopped
- 2 pcs Chinese celery stalks, sliced into 1-inch pieces

Instructions:

1. Boil enough water in a steamer pot or wok on medium high. Place a steamer tray, big enough to carry the fish, making sure the boiling water does not touch the bottom of the tray.

2. Stuff lemongrass stalks into the cavity of the fish and carefully place in the steamer tray.

3. Cover with a tight fitting lid and steam vigorously for about 15 minutes.

4. Meanwhile, heat chicken stock in a pan on medium fire.

5. Once it starts boiling, add the palm sugar and stir to dissolve. Transfer to a bowl and set aside.

6. In another bowl, combine garlic, chilies, and cilantro with lime juice and fish sauce.

7. To serve, scatter Chinese celery stalks in a serving platter.

8. Place the fish on top, drizzle with prepared sauce, and serve with the soup on the side.

Steamed Shellfish Pot

If it is becoming a challenge to choose what seafood to steam, you can simply make a selection of your favorite shellfish and toss them all together into the pot. The steamer can host different types of seafood, and shellfish taste incredibly good when they are cooked in gentle steam.

Serving Size: 6

Prep Time: 35 mins

Ingredients:

- 1 lb. live crawfish
- ½ lb. shrimps
- ½ lb. scallops
- 12 pcs mussels
- 12 pcs little neck clams
- ½ lb. sausage, smoked and sliced into rounds
- 4 pcs large potatoes, peeled and sliced into quarters
- 6 pcs small onions, peeled
- 4 garlic cloves, crushed
- 2 bottles clam juice
- 3 cups dry white wine
- ¾ cup Old Bay seasoning

Instructions:

1. Combine clam juice, wine, and enough water at the bottom of a steamer pot.

2. Let it boil mixture on medium fire.

3. Place the steamer basket on top of the pot and add potatoes. Let it steam with the lid on for about 5 minutes.

4. Add crawfish, whole onions, and crushed garlic. Then, cover again and continue to steam for another 10 minutes.

5. Add shrimps, scallops, mussels, clams, and sausages into the steamer basket, sprinkle with Old Bay seasoning, and steam for another 5 minutes with the lid on.

6. Spread out the steamed shellfish selection into a serving platter.

7. Spoon broth into individual bowls for serving.

Steamed Lemon-Garlic Chicken

We have steamed breakfast, steamed veggies, and steamed seafood. So, what's next? You guessed right, meat! This is a section for meat lovers. Believe it or not, meats can sit well with the steamer as much as your veggies and seafood can. This Steamed Lemon-Garlic Chicken, for example, is a breath of fresh air. It tastes as delightful, but the flavor of the meat is fuller and a lot cleaner. Want to know what we mean by that? Let's start with the recipe.

Serving Size: 2

Prep Time: 25 mins

Ingredients:

- 2 pcs skinless and boneless chicken breasts
- Juice and zest of 1 pc lemon
- 2 cloves garlic, minced
- 2 pcs fresh thyme sprigs, chopped
- 1/8 tsp red chili flakes
- Sea salt and freshly ground black pepper to taste

Instructions:

1. Boil enough water in a steamer pot over medium fire.

2. Meanwhile, sprinkle some salt and pepper onto chicken breasts.

3. Rub with garlic, lemon zest, and chili flakes all over.

4. Place a sheet of parchment paper in a steamer basket and arrange the chicken breasts.

5. Add thyme sprigs on top.

6. Put the steamer basket on top of the boiling water in the pot. Cover and steam for about 10 minutes.

7. Arrange steamed chicken in a serving platter, squeeze in lemon juice all over, and serve with a garnish of more freshly chopped thyme sprigs on top.

Steamed Beef with Oyster Sauce

You are used to beefing stir fry and consider it one of the most amazing dinner recipes that everyone in the family looks forward to. But next time you are tinkering about the idea of serving beef stir fry, substitute with this steamed beef instead. This is a delightful, if not more, and healthier, too.

Serving Size: 5

Prep Time: 25 mins

Ingredients:

- 1 lb. beef sirloin, thinly sliced
- 6 pcs pechay Baguio
- 1 pc carrot, thinly sliced
- 1 pc red bell pepper, thinly sliced
- 2 tbsp green onions, chopped
- 1 tsp ginger, grated
- 2 tbsp oyster sauce
- 1 tbsp Chinese cooking wine
- 1 tbsp oyster sauce
- 1 tsp Sriracha sauce
- 2 tsp sesame oil
- 2 tbsp rice flour
- ½ tsp baking soda
- 3 pcs star anise
- ½ tsp salt

Instructions:

1. Stir together cooking wine, oyster sauce, Sriracha sauce, and sesame oil plus green onions, ginger, and baking soda in a large bowl until well blended.

2. Add beef strips and mix to coat, then, cover bowl with plastic wrap and store in the fridge for about 30 minutes to marinade.

3. After 30 minutes, remove beef from the marinade and toss with rice flour until well coated.

4. Boil enough water in a steamer pot over medium fire.

5. Arrange pechay Baguio leaves in a steamer basket, add beef slices, plus carrots and bell peppers.

6. Steam with the lid on for about 5 minutes.

7. Toss beef with oyster sauce and place in a serving platter.

8. Serve and enjoy.

Steamed Pork Ribs and Pumpkin

It's a delightful made with pork and pumpkin, and of course, the steamer. It's a healthy and tasty dish that the entire family will love, what with a hint of sweetness in tender-juicy, mouthwatering pork ribs.

Serving Size: 2

Prep Time: 35 mins

Ingredients:

- ½ lb. pork short ribs, cut into 2-inch pieces
- 2 cups pumpkin, cubed
- 2 pcs green onion stalks, chopped
- 1 tbsp oyster sauce
- ½ tbsp soy sauce
- ½ tbsp cornstarch
- ¼ tsp sugar
- ½ tsp salt

Instructions:

1. Whisk together oyster and soy sauce, plus cornstarch, sugar, and salt in a large bowl.

2. Add pork ribs and stir to coat. Set aside and let it marinade in the fridge for at least 10 minutes or longer.

3. When the pork is almost ready, boil enough water in a steamer pot over medium fire.

4. Place the marinated pork ribs in a heat-proof dish together with pumpkin cubes.

5. Carefully place the dish into the steamer basket, cover, and steam for 20 minutes.

6. After steaming, transfer pork and pumpkin into a serving platter, garnish with freshly chopped green onions, and serve.

Steamed Meat Dumplings

Meat dumplings are delightful. There's no question to that. You can serve them fried or baked, nothing beats steaming, still. It remains to be the best cooking method for preparing dumplings, keeping them moist and tasty, sans the need of too much grease.

Serving Size: 4

Prep Time: 1 hr. 10 mins

Ingredients:

- 48 pcs siu mai wrappers
- ½ lb. ground pork
- ½ lb. ground pork sausage
- ½ cup water chestnuts, minced
- ½ cup mushrooms, minced
- ¼ cup coriander, minced
- 1 cup green onions, finely chopped
- 1 tsp fresh ginger, peeled and grated
- 1 tbsp sherry
- 1 tsp teriyaki sauce
- 3 tbsp soy sauce
- 1 tsp sesame oil
- 1 tbsp salad oil
- 1 pc egg white
- 1 ½ tbsp cornstarch
- 1 tsp sugar
- ½ tsp salt

Instructions:

1. Mix all the ingredients together in a large bowl, except for wrappers and salad oil, to make the filling.

2. Place a teaspoon of mixture in the center of a wrapper, gather up and carefully seal the sides.

3. Brush the dumplings with salad oil, then, arrange in a steamer basket.

4. Boil enough water in a steamer pot over medium fire, then, place the steamer basket with the dumplings.

5. Steam with the lid on for about 20 minutes.

6. Serve with your favorite dipping sauce and enjoy.

Steamed Minced Pork

This steamed minced pork recipe is just like another version of the steamed meat dumplings. This time, however, the meat is not enclosed in a wrapper. And it is also on another level, with salted fish and preserved cabbage mixed with pork. This is a delightful dish that you can serve with a bowl of congee or hot, steamed rice and enjoy every spoonful.

Serving Size: 5

Prep Time: 15 mins

Ingredients:

- ½ lb. lean ground pork
- 2 tbsp salted fish, minced
- 1 tbsp preserved cabbage, minced
- 2 pcs water chestnuts, peeled and minced finely
- 1 tbsp ginger, peeled and grated
- 2 pcs shallots, peeled and minced
- 1 garlic clove, minced
- 3 pcs spring onion stalks, finely chopped and divided
- 1 pc red chilli, seeded and sliced
- 1 pc egg yolk
- 1 tbsp light soy sauce
- ½ tsp dark soy sauce
- 2 tbsp shallot oil

Instructions:

1. Combine pork soy sauce, and sesame oil in a large bowl.

2. Stir in flour, plus salt and pepper until well blended.

3. Add salted fish, preserved cabbage, water chestnuts, ginger, shallots, garlic, half of the spring onions, and egg yolk. Mix to incorporate.

4. Transfer mixture to a lightly greased heatproof bowl, forming into a patty, with about 1 inch allowance from the edge of the bowl.

5. Boil enough water in a steamer pot over medium fire.

6. Place the bowl with minced pork in the steamer tray, cover with a lid, and let it steam for about 12 minutes or until the meat is cooked through.

7. Meanwhile, stir together light and dark soy sauce, plus shallot oil in a small bowl.

8. Drizzle over minced pork, garnish with the remaining spring onions and chili, then, serve and enjoy.

Chinese-Style Steamed Chicken

There is a reason steaming is highly preferred in most Chinese kitchens. This cooking method helps to keep the food moist and tender. The taste and texture are always excellent. That is very true in this steamed chicken recipe with lots of ginger and green onions. It is simple, quick, and easy to make yet extravagant in terms of taste, especially if you serve it with a delicious soy-based sauce.

Serving Size: 2

Prep Time: 30 mins

Ingredients:

- ½ of 1 chicken whole
- 1 tbsp ginger, peeled and grated
- 1 tbsp green onions, thinly sliced
- 1 tsp Chinese cooking wine
- 1 tbsp light soy sauce
- ½ tsp salt

For the Dipping Sauce:

- 1 tbsp green onions, chopped
- 1 clove garlic, minced
- 1 tbsp sesame oil
- 1 tbsp oyster sauce
- 1 tbsp light soy sauce
- 4 tbsp water

Instructions:

1. Whisk together cooking wine, soy sauce, and salt in a small bowl.

2. Pour marinade into chicken, rubbing all sides evenly. Set aside for about 30 minutes.

3. When chicken is almost ready, boil enough water in the steamer pot over medium fire.

4. Lay down chicken in a heatproof dish, cover top with ginger and green onions, and place it in a steamer basket on top of the boiling water. Cover and let steam on high for half an hour.

5. For the dipping sauce, heat oil in a saucepan on medium and sauté garlic and green onions until fragrant.

6. Stir in oyster and soy sauce, plus water, and let it simmer for 2 minutes.

7. Serve chicken with the prepared sauce on the side.

Steamed Carrot Cake

A carrot cake is another delicious recipe that you can unbelievably make with the steamer. It's a very clean and healthy dessert with a little bit of spice of a savory difference. Try this at home. You and the kids will surely enjoy it.

Serving Size: 6

Prep Time: 1 hr. 20 mins

Ingredients:

- 1 ½ cups carrots, peeled and finely grated
- ¼ tsp baking soda
- 1 tbsp fresh ginger, peeled and finely grated
- ½ cup raisins
- ½ tsp baking powder
- ¼ tsp fine salt
- ¾ cup dark brown sugar
- ¾ cup all-purpose flour
- ¼ tsp ground black pepper
- 4 tsp honey
- 1 pc large egg yolk
- 1 pc large egg
- 6 tbsp vegetable oil
- ½ tsp ground cinnamon
- Cooking spray

Instructions:

1. Prepare lightly greased ramekins. Set aside.

2. Whisk together carrots, ginger, brown sugar, honey, egg, egg yolk, and oil until well blended.

3. In another bowl, sift together baking soda, salt, flour, cinnamon, baking powder, and pepper.

4. Gradually stir in the dry ingredients into the carrots mixture.

5. Fold in the raisins and mix to blend.

6. Divide the batter between the prepared ramekins, then, arrange the ramekins in a steamer tray.

7. Boil enough water in a steamer pot on medium fire.

8. Place the steamer tray with the ramekins, cover, and steam for about 40 minutes or until a toothpick inserted in the middle comes clean.

9. Let the carrot cakes cool a little before serving.

Steamed Sponge Cake

If you think you cannot make a cake just because you don't have an oven, think again. Your steamer will do, believe it or not. This Steamed Sponge Cake recipe will prove to you that having a steamer could be enough to make a yummy cake that the whole family can enjoy.

Serving Size: 4

Prep Time: 1 hr. 25 mins

Ingredients:

- 1 ½ cups all-purpose flour
- ½ cup butter, softened
- 1 tbsp custard powder
- 1 tsp baking soda
- 1 ½ cups brown sugar
- 4 tbsp melon seeds, roasted
- 4 tbsp chocolate sauce
- 1 tsp soda
- 1 tbsp honey
- 1 tsp vanilla extract
- 3 pcs eggs
- 6 tbsp corn oil

Instructions:

1. Stir together flour, custard powder, baking soda, and soda in a bowl. Set aside.

2. Cream butter and sugar in another bowl.

3. Add corn oil and stir.

4. Gradually add eggs, one at a time, stirring the mixture with every addition.

5. Pour in honey and vanilla and mix until well blended.

6. Add flour mixture into the butter mixture slowly until incorporated.

7. Fold in melon seeds and stir.

8. Pour batter in a lightly greased dish and place the dish in a steamer basket.

9. Boil enough water in a steamer pot on medium fire, then, place the steamer basket into the pot and let the cake steam for about 45 minutes or until a toothpick inserted in the middle of the cake comes out clean.

10. Let the cake cool down a little before removing from the dish.

11. Garnish with chocolate sauce and more roasted melon seeds.

Steamed Chocolate Cake

Chocolate cake is everybody's favorite comfort food. And it is so comforting that you can make a chocolate cake with the steamer. Try this version, and you will see that there is very little difference with the conventional one. Some people even impressed that this steamed version is a lot more interesting!

Serving Size: 8

Prep Time: 1 hr. 25 mins

Ingredients:

- 1 cup chocolate ganache
- ½ cup cocoa powder
- 1 cup plain flour
- ½ tsp baking soda
- ½ tsp baking powder
- 1 cup caster sugar
- 2 tbsp rum
- 1 cup evaporated milk
- 2 pcs eggs, lightly beaten
- ¾ cup butter
- ½ tsp vanilla extract

Instructions:

1. Melt butter in a pan on low fire.

2. Add milk, vanilla, and sugar, stirring constantly until the sugar is dissolved. Set aside to cool down.

3. When the butter mixture is cool enough, whisk in eggs and rum.

4. Meanwhile, stir together baking soda, flour, cocoa powder, and baking powder in a large bowl

5. Gradually pour flour mixture into the butter mixture, stirring to form a batter.

6. Transfer cake batter into a lightly greased round baking pan.

7. Boil enough water in a steamer pot on medium fire, then, place the cake in a steamer basket on top.

8. Let the cake steam for about 50 minutes or until a toothpick inserted in the middle of the cake comes out clean. Set aside to cool down before removing the cake from the pan.

9. When the cake is cool enough, pour chocolate ganache onto the cake and smoother with a spatula.

10. Chill the cake in the fridge for a few minutes before serving.

Conclusion

Steaming is one of the greatest of the cooking methods! Treating your food with hot steam to enjoy the moist and tender dish, whether it's just plain eggs or veggies or seafood or meat. And believe it or not, you can do this even to a cake!

This cookbook will allow you to see how important having a steamer around the house is. You should invest in one, a good quality one, which will allow you to create many delicious meals that the entire family can enjoy. You can steam food for breakfast, lunch, dinner, and even for dessert. There is really no limit as to the kind of dishes that you can make in the steamer. A lot of the meals that you cook by other means – baking, boiling, poaching, sautéing – can be transformed into a steamed recipe. So, the options are practically limitless.

Once you get the heck of it, you will surely enjoy steaming and would love to steam whenever possible. Steaming is wonderful, especially when you do it with veggies. You do not only make them healthier by omitting any possible use of grease but also make their colors brighter. Steamed veggies are perfect for your side dishes. But steamed seafood is also as delightful, if not more. Any of your fresh catch will surely taste even better if you pop them into the steamer. You can simply eat them as is or with a dipping sauce or some special concoction to drizzle all over.

Anything you put in the steamer basically tastes great, so you should not limit yourself to just one ingredient or recipe.

Happy cooking!

About the Author

Molly Mills always knew she wanted to feed people delicious food for a living. Being the oldest child with three younger brothers, Molly learned to prepare meals at an early age to help out her busy parents. She just seemed to know what spice went with which meat and how to make sauces that would dress up the blandest of pastas. Her creativity in the kitchen was a blessing to a family where money was tight and making new meals every day was a challenge.

Molly was also a gifted athlete as well as chef and secured a Lacrosse scholarship to Syracuse University. This was a blessing to her family as she was the first to go to college and at little cost to her parents. She took full advantage of her college education and earned a business degree. When she graduated, she joined her culinary skills and business acumen into a successful catering business. She wrote her first e-book after a customer asked if she could pay for several of her recipes. This sparked the entrepreneurial spirit in Mills and she thought if one person wanted them, then why not share the recipes with the world!

Molly lives near her family's home with her husband and three children and still cooks for her family every chance she gets. She plays Lacrosse with a local team made up of her old teammates from college and there are always some tasty nibbles on the ready after each game.

Don't Miss Out!

Scan the QR-Code below and you can sign up to receive emails whenever Molly Mills publishes a new book. There's no charge and no obligation.

Sign Me Up

https://molly.gr8.com

Printed in Great Britain
by Amazon